Starter Book 4

Tunes in $\frac{2}{4}$ $\frac{3}{4}$ $\frac{4}{4}$ and $\frac{2}{2}$ (simple times)

used these notes   **and these rests**

crotchets   1 beat

pairs of quavers $\frac{1}{2}$ beats

groups of 4 quavers $\frac{1}{2}$ beats

dotted crotchets $1\frac{1}{2}$ beats

and

single quavers $\frac{1}{2}$ beat

minims   2 beats

dotted minims   3 beats

semibreves   4 beats

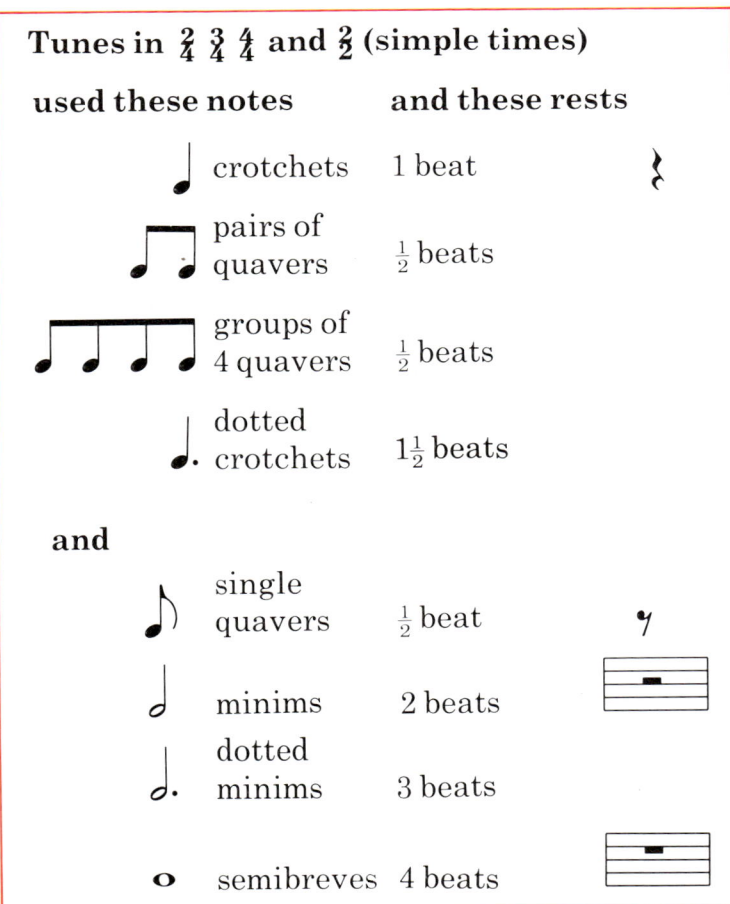

Tunes in $\frac{6}{8}$ (compound time) used

dotted crotchet beats

divided into

a crotchet and a quaver

three quavers

or

a crotchet and a quaver rest

and also

dotted minims 2 beats in compound time

and

a dotted crotchet tied to a crotchet $1\frac{2}{3}$ beats (five quavers)

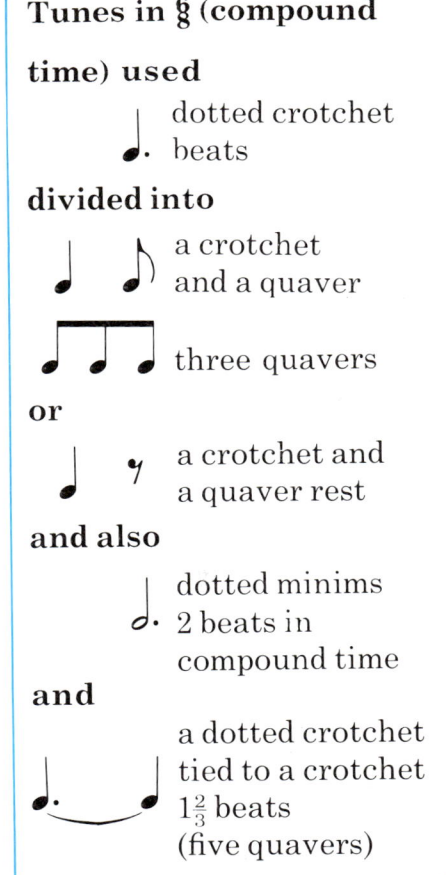

You played tunes in these keys

C major

G major

D major

A major

A minor

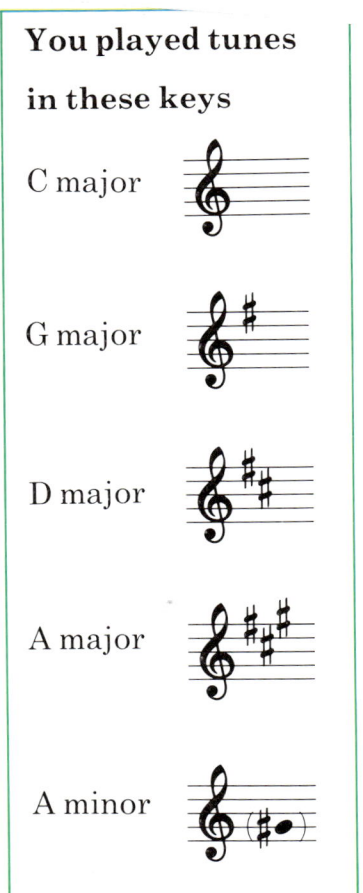

1

Twist and Stretch

Play low D gently.
Now try to cover the lowest double hole
with your little finger.
If your finger is too short,
twist and turn the foot joint of your recorder
so that your finger can sit comfortably over the double hole.
You will find it easier if you stretch out the ring fingers
of both hands well across the recorder.

Now tongue, very very gently, into the recorder.
Say 'dooooo' instead of 'tooooo' to give a nice round sound.

If there are squeaks, check for leaks, or blow even more gently.

If all the holes are covered properly then the sound you are playing is **low C**.

C

To play low C,
cover all the holes
like this:

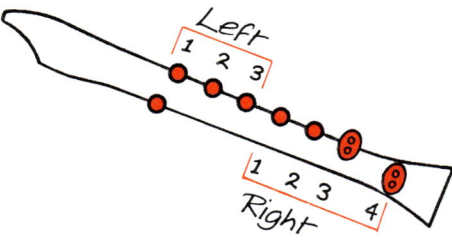

To write low C,
draw a small line
just below the stave
and put a note on it,
like this:

I'm a
leger line

Softee Mix

Low notes need very little breath.
Low C is a real 'softee'.
Make up 'softee' tunes
with the low notes.
Mix E, D and C into different tunes.
Don't blow too hard
or you'll melt the ice-cream!

When the 'softee' mix is ready,
push in a chocolate flake,
or squeeze over some raspberry sauce,
by adding some higher notes.

Home to C

Whispering waves

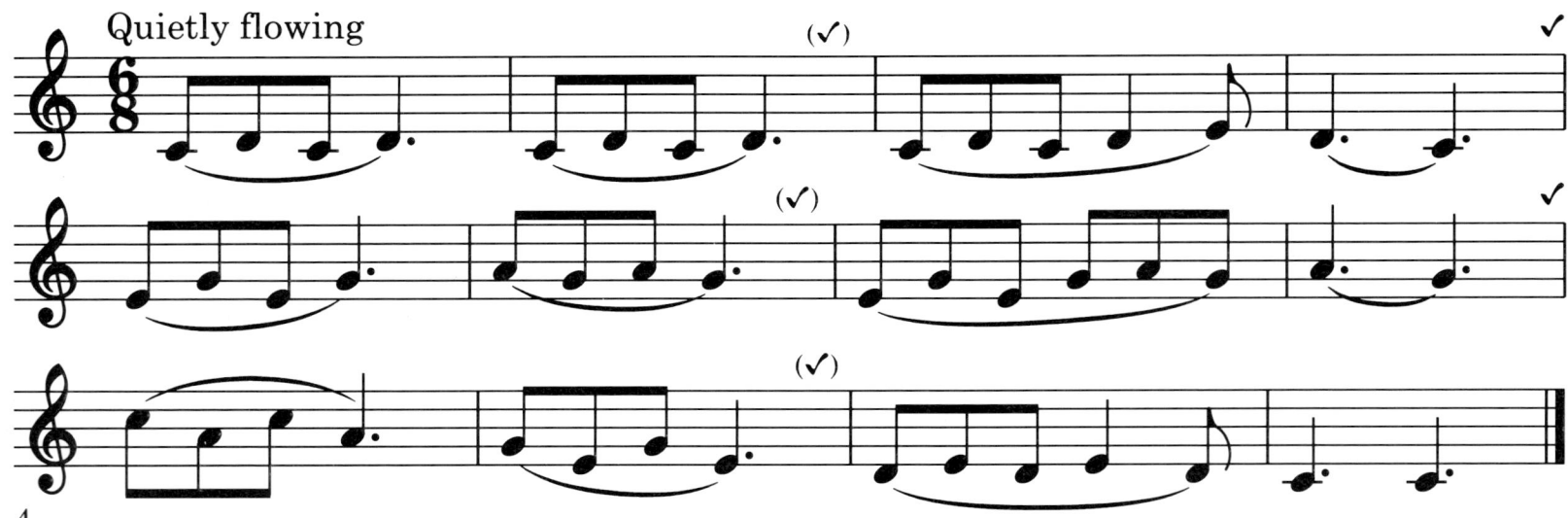

Dolphins and whales

Slow

Pass one window

With a swing

Over the hills and far away

Traditional Scottish
(used in the Beggar's Opera)

Not too fast

6

Maa bonny lad

Northumbrian folksong

Fairly slow

We wish you a merry Christmas

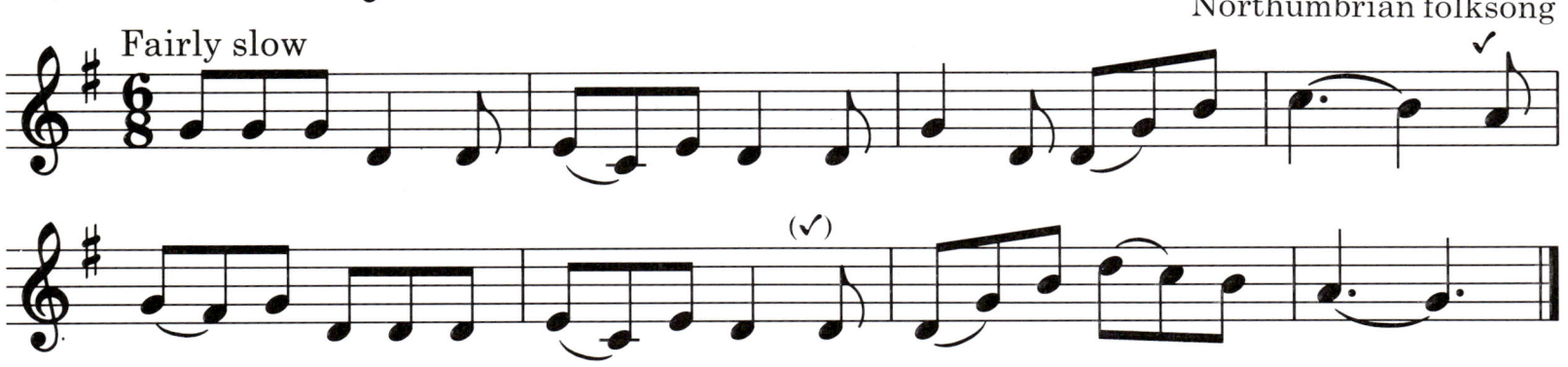

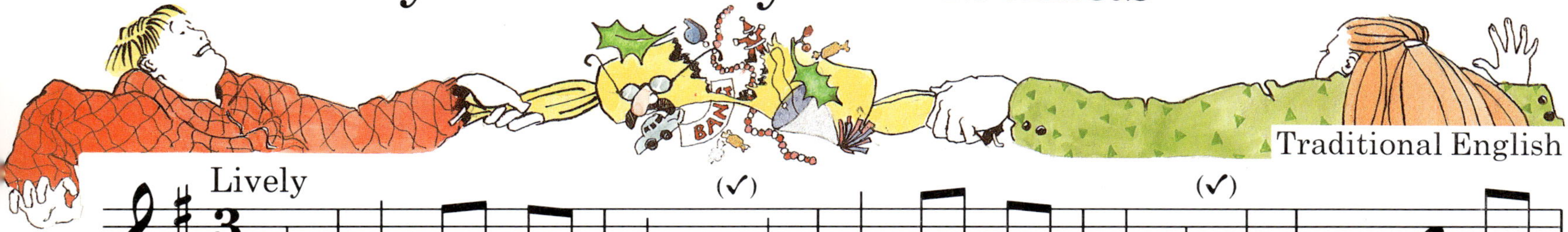

Traditional English

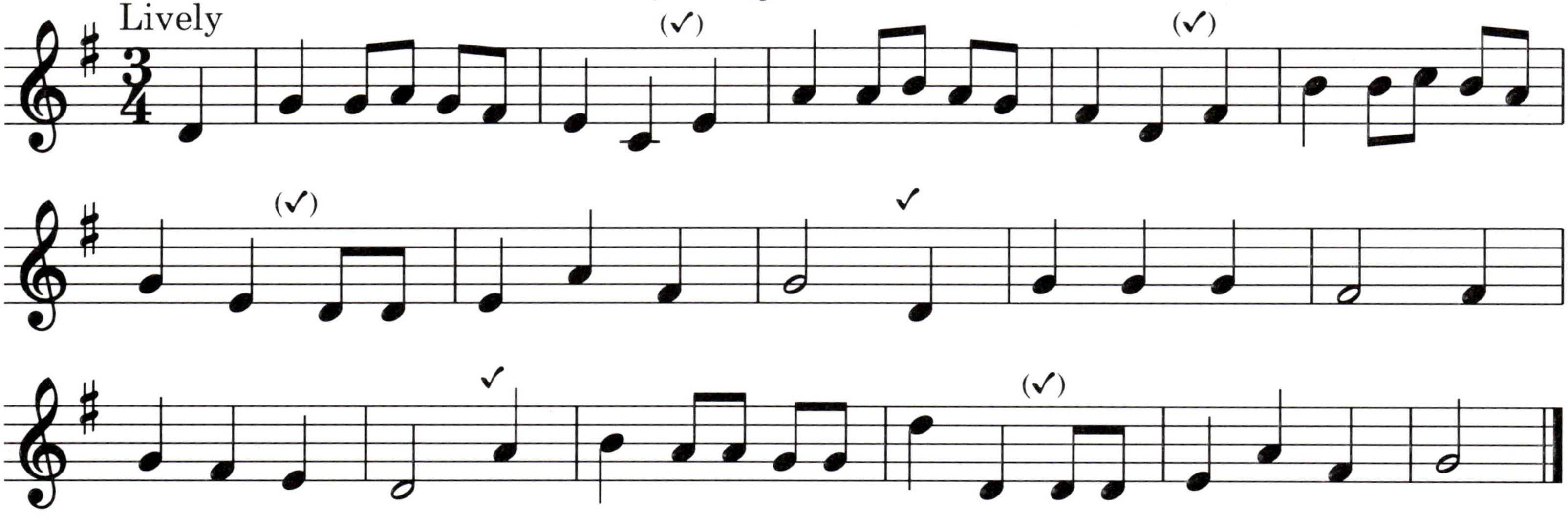
Lively

Plain F or F natural (F♮) is a semitone lower than F sharp.

To play F natural, finger low C but lift off the middle finger of your right hand, like this:

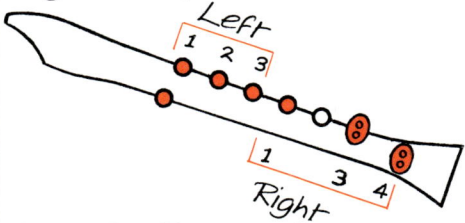

To write F natural, put a note in the bottom space, like this:

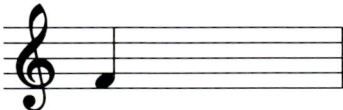

There is no need to add the natural sign, but always play F natural unless there is an accidental, or a sharp in the key signature.

Micro Mix

When you play your recorder you must listen hard to check that you are playing in tune. The amount of breath makes a lot of difference.

Too much breath, and the sound might be too high or *sharp*. Too little, and the sound might be too low or *flat*.

In most music, a semitone is the smallest interval, but some composers and musicians like to 'bend' a sound up or down, with microtones.

Here is a chance to experiment with some microtones. Between G and E there are a number of different Fs. Here are their fingerings.

nearly F♯	**really F♯**	nasty F♮	nearly F♮	**really F♮**

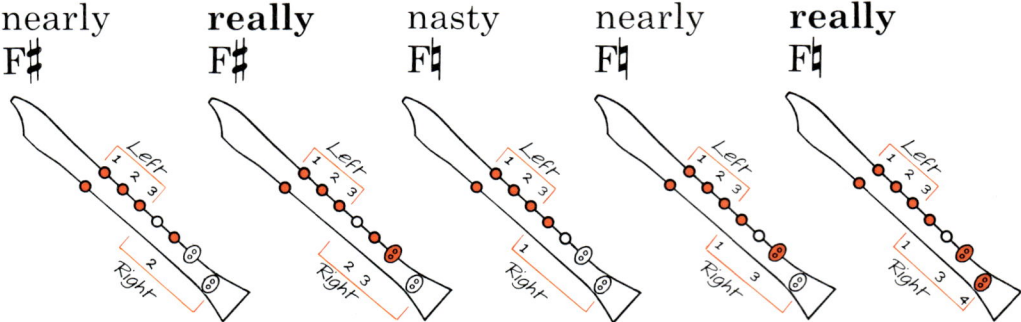

Try them, and then use your imagination to make up a **micro mix piece** by using them for moans and groans and other special effects.

Vary the fingerings and the breath pressure – you'll be surprised at some of the sounds you find.

The scale of C major

Now that you know low C and F natural you will be able to play a scale of C.
On a keyboard, the scale of C uses just white notes.
Remember on the recorder to play F natural, not F sharp.
Practise playing the scale up and down.

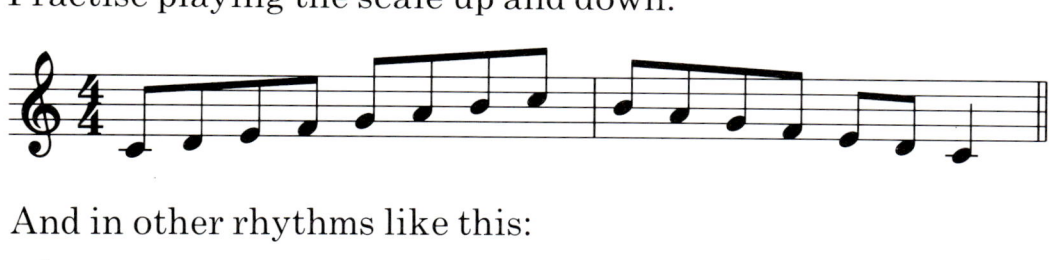

And in other rhythms like this:

Try repeating some notes to make it more like a tune.

Oats and beans

9

Hand-cart song

American folksong

Caterpillar here, caterpillar there

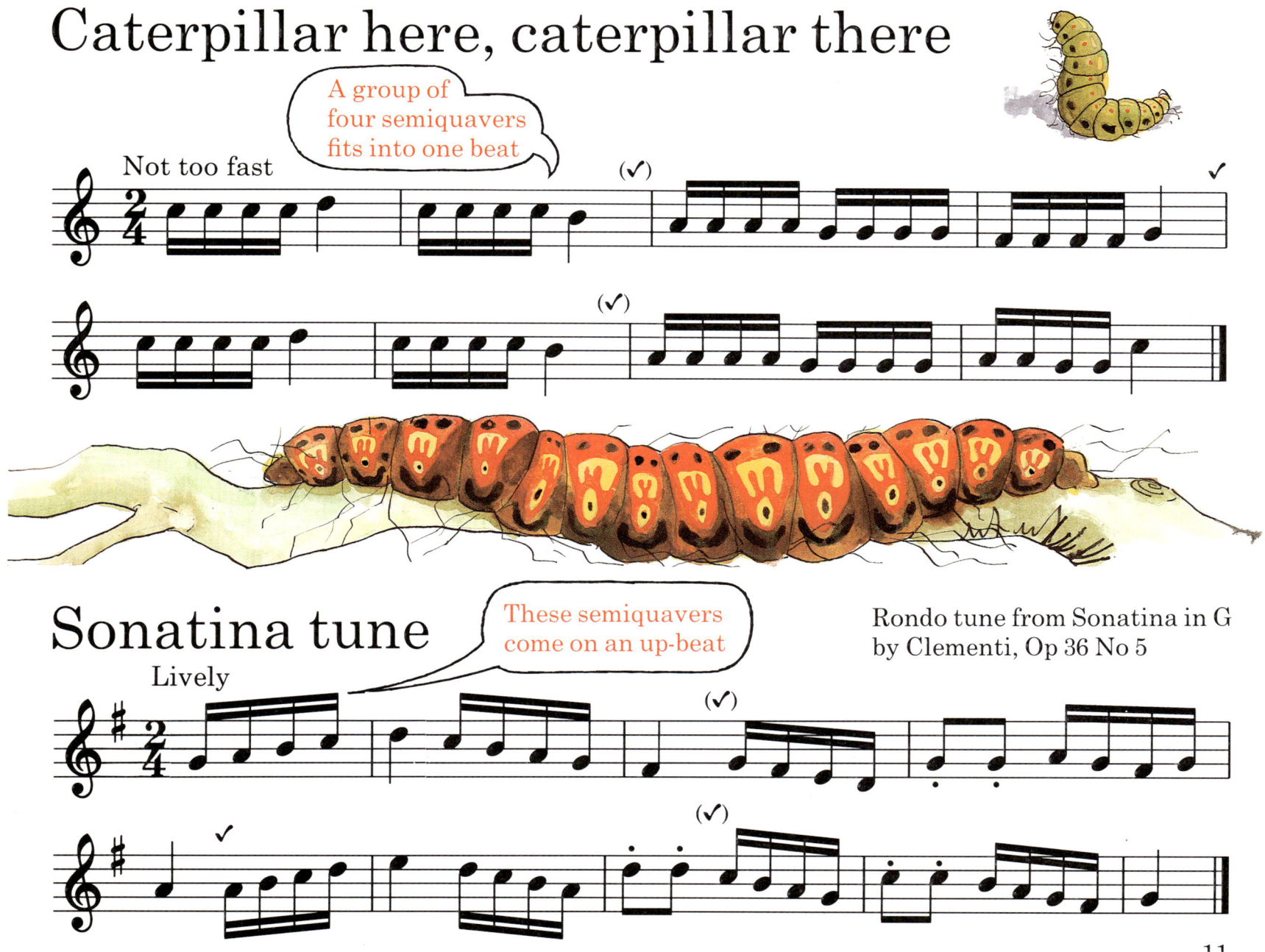

Helicopter pad

With care

1st part

2nd part

12

What shall we do with the drunken sailor?

English capstan shanty

13

Green grow the rushes, O!

Traditional English

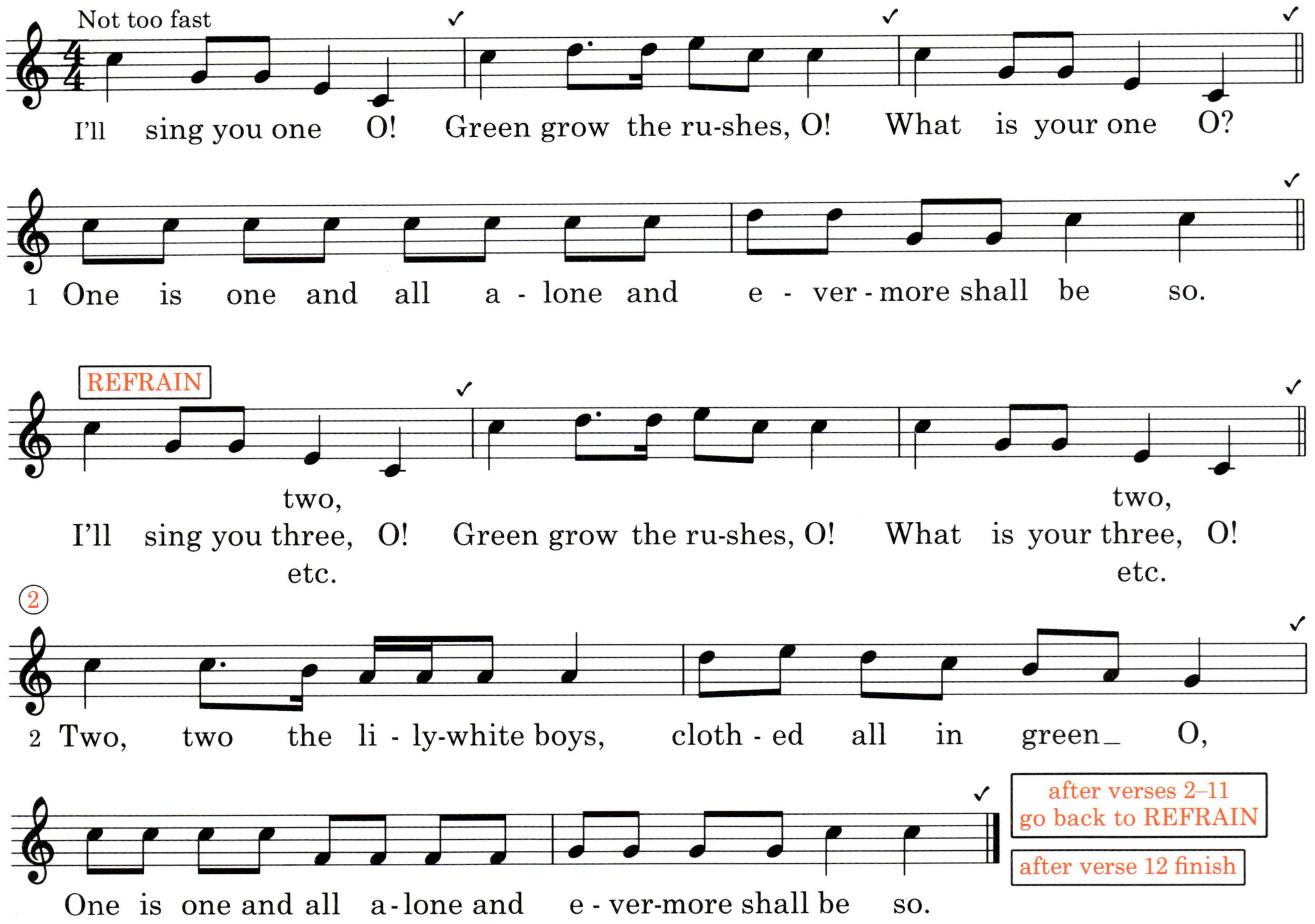

Not too fast

I'll sing you one O! Green grow the ru-shes, O! What is your one O?

1 One is one and all a - lone and e - ver - more shall be so.

REFRAIN

two,

I'll sing you three, O! Green grow the ru-shes, O! What is your three, O!

etc.

two,

etc.

② 2 Two, two the li - ly-white boys, cloth - ed all in green_ O,

after verses 2–11 go back to REFRAIN

after verse 12 finish

One is one and all a-lone and e - ver-more shall be so.

14

③

♪ Three, three the ri - vals, *to 2*

④ to ⑫

in verse 5, 7 and 11 only, play the small notes and then the next bar

4 Four for the gos - pel ma - kers, *to 3 (and then to 2)*
5 Five for the sym - bols at your door and Four for the gos - pel ma - kers, *to 3*
6 Six for six proud walk - ers, *to 5*
7 Seven for the seven stars in the sky and Six for the six proud walk - ers, *to 5*
8 Eight for the Ap - ril rain - ers, *to 7*
9 Nine for the nine bright shin - ers, *to 8*
10 Ten for the ten com - mand - ments, *to 9*
11 Eleven for the eleven went up to heav'n, and Ten for the ten com - mand - ments, *to 9*
12 Twelve for the twelve A - post - les, *to 11*

F′

To play top F,
finger F natural,
lift up the little finger
and pinch the thumb-hole,
like this:

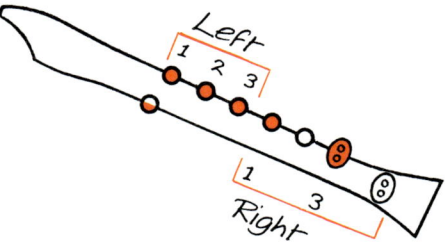

To write top F put a note
on the top line like this:

Two rounds

To play these rounds in parts divide into groups.
One group starts, and when it has played two bars the next
group joins in from the beginning. Carry on until all groups
are playing. Repeat the music several times. To end, either
'fade out' one part at a time, or finish all together when one
part reaches the last note of the melody.

The moon and me

French

Great Tom is cast

English

Rigadon

Purcell

Lively

1st part

Play A in repeat

2nd part

Auld lang syne

Traditional Scottish

Key of F major

Pieces which end
on F are usually in
the key of F major.
This key uses B flat
in place of B natural.
The key signature for
F major has a single flat
on the middle line.

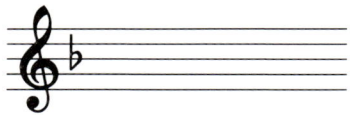

You can learn how
to play B flat on page 20.

Steady

The Sunshine Special

Negro revivalist song

Play A to lead into 2nd part

1st part

2nd part

B♭

B flat is a semitone lower
than B natural.
To finger B flat,
close the thumb-hole
as usual then use the
first and third fingers
of the left hand and
the first right hand finger:

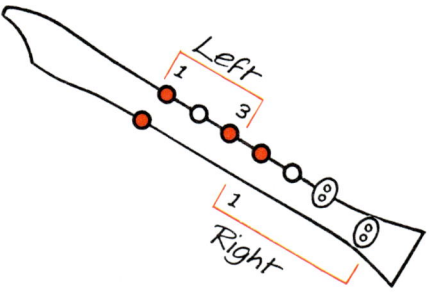

To write B flat put a note
on the middle line with
a sign for a flat in front:

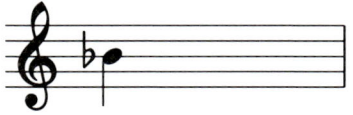

Natural, Flat and Sharp Mix

You now know two forms of the notes B, C, F and G.
By lowering B to B flat, or raising F, C or G with
a sharp you can change the character of a tune greatly.
Sadder, brighter, darker, lighter.

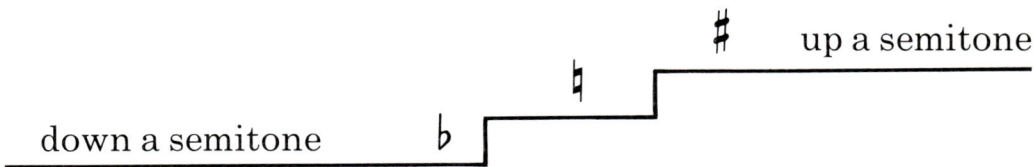

See how many ways you can alter this tune with the
sharps or flats that you know. Bars 1, 2 and 4 can be changed
in one way only, but there are lots and lots of ways
to change bar 3.

When you have experimented with the tune above,
make up one of your own. It must have at least
one B, C, F or G to make flat or sharp.

Remember you also know two forms of top F.
Perhaps you could include this note to play as a sharp or natural?

The scale of F major

Now that you know the note B flat you will be able to play the scale of F major.

As with the scales you know already, practise it up and down and in different rhythms.

This old man

Traditional English

1st part

Lively

2nd part

Keep that wheel a-turning

English folksong 'William Brown'

Not too fast

Round review

When you play this short piece you will revise all the notes you know so far.
If you play it as a round with a partner, two of you can revise your notes at the same time!

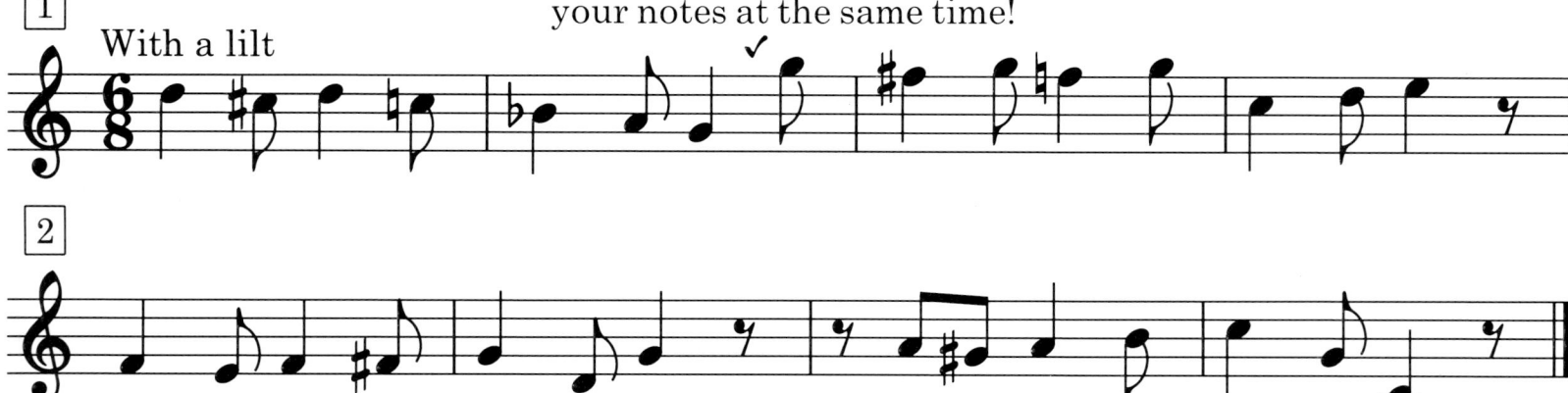

22

Melodic scale of D minor

Minor scales are of two kinds, *melodic* and *harmonic*.
In the melodic form the sixth and seventh notes
are lowered a semitone when the scale is downward.

In the harmonic form they remain the same,
a tone and a half apart. In D minor they are B♭ and C♯ .

Charlie is my darling

Traditional
Scottish

Da Capo (D.C.) means:
from the beginning or 'head'.
Al Fine (pronounced *feenay*)
means: to the finish or end.

Da Capo
al Fine

23

O rare Turpin hero

English folksong

B flat Bugle Mix

Bugle or trumpet calls are a way of giving instructions, or of showing who is calling. Here is a well-known example:

Do you know what it tells you to do?

Trumpet calls use just the notes B♭, D and F.
Mix these notes together to make your own calls.
You might like to include top F in some.